Contents

---

[1] 'Staff' and 'adult' have been used in this guideline to include all adults working with the children.

Foreword

The provision of high quality pre-school education is a priority for us all. High quality pre-school education enriches children's early years experiences and helps children to acquire the skills, knowledge and positive dispositions required for effective and useful learning. As a result, the benefits can carry through to the start of formal education, and even beyond, into lifelong learning.

Information and communications technologies (ICT) are an integral part of our lives today. Interest and confidence in engaging with ICT resources in their many forms are necessary so that all of us are able to play a full part in society. This is as important for young children as it is for young people and adults.

These technologies can be powerful tools for enhancing young children's learning. This Policy sets out the framework within which this learning can take place and outlines how adults can assist in this process. Combined with the support of the other elements of the ICT Strategy for Early Years that are outlined in this document, we can help children get the most from learning with and through ICT in their early years.

Euan Robson

Deputy Minister for Education and Young People

The ICT Strategy for Early Years

The ICT[2] strategy for early years has four components:

- the document *Early Learning, Forward Thinking: The Policy Framework for Early Years* sets out the framework and background to the ICT strategy for early years. It is based around principles from the *Curriculum Framework for Children 3 to 5* and explores the aims to which we need to be working. It reflects on the relevance of ICT in the early years context and provides an overview of effective use of technologies in this setting

- a programme of training and support for the early years workforce will deliver a pool of trainers in each local authority area who will work to drive forward professional development for all members of the workforce in relation to ICT

- a range of support and guidance materials for early years staff. Current good practice both here and abroad will be shared and case studies used to inform the delivery of the policy framework.

- a process of monitoring and evaluation to appraise the impact of the strategy.

Rationale

Young children come to early years settings as active, experienced learners with a natural curiosity. They are unique individuals eager to make sense of their world, to develop relationships and to extend their skills.

A Curriculum Framework for Children 3 to 5, Scottish CCC, 1999

Rapid developments in information and communications technologies are already instrumental in producing an ever-changing and fast-evolving world. The current generation of young children are children of the information age, living in a world rich in media resources. Their natural curiosity and enthusiasm often leads to them taking advantage of increased opportunities for interactions with information and communications technologies in their homes and communities. Early years educators must recognise these developments and build upon the individual experiences that young children bring with them.

In order for adults to both enhance children's learning and to help them to develop dispositions and attitudes which will be of value to them both now and in the future, early years educators must further develop their own enthusiasm for and confidence in using ICT.

Background to the Strategy

The use of ICT has been established in primary and secondary schools for a number of years now. The benefits of using ICT have been well documented for primary and secondary pupils (Condie et al., 2002; DfES/Becta, 2002; Harris and Kington, 2002) in terms of improved motivation, enthusiasm, task management, subject knowledge and of course improved ICT skills. There is evidence (DfES/Becta, 2002) to suggest a correlation between 'good ICT resources' and improved attainment. Increased availability of resources and staff training has encouraged rapid developments in the use of ICT in schools.

---

[2] 'ICT' has been used to indicate the wide range of information and communications technologies that can be used in early years settings.

Although some ICT resources have been used in early years settings[3] for many years, for instance the use of video and audio equipment and limited computer resources, there is likely to be discontinuity in terms of children's experiences with ICT when they move on from their early years setting into primary school. The ICT strategy for early years is intended to redress the balance.

The Purpose of this Policy Framework

This policy framework provides details on how information and communications technologies can enhance and support the development and learning of children aged 3–5 years, providing them with a secure foundation upon which they can build. The framework will also inform the planning and delivery of professional development in relation to the potential uses of ICT, for all those involved in the implementation of early years services.

ICT in the Early Years Setting

Although ICT is often equated with the use of desktop computers, it is important, when considering the needs of young children, to adopt a wide-ranging definition of what is meant by ICT. It is clear, from looking at children's lives at home and in the community, that ICT is presently often embedded in their everyday experiences, for example in bar codes in supermarkets, interactive television programmes, microwave ovens, vacuum cleaners, video/DVD players and traffic lights at pedestrian crossings. These experiences are likely to be qualitatively different from those offered in the early years setting. Some children may not only be aware of ICT around them, but also interested in how devices work even before they start attending their early years setting. On the other hand, others will have little knowledge or experience.

ICT resources for young children have characteristics of communication and interactivity:
- communicating information such as:
  - digital still and video cameras
  - audiocassettes
  - video/DVD/TV
  - internet
  - mobile phones
  - e-mail
- promoting interactivity such as:
  - programmable toys and robots
  - musical keyboards
  - activity centres
  - digital interactive TV
  - children's websites
  - remote controlled toys.

Learning *about* ICT involves developing skills in various aspects of technology. Computer analogies would be learning how to use a mouse or learning how to start programs.

---

[3] 'Early years setting' has been used to describe the range of different types of provision, including playgroups, nursery classes, nursery schools, etc.

Learning *with* and *through* ICT however involves using them as tools for learning. Some computer analogies would be using software programs to explore music or accessing information from the internet.

Learning with ICT can:

- enhance present learning, with the use of sensitive feedback and dynamic presentation
- support and extend children's development
- assist children to generalise concepts and skills
- engage children in self-directed learning.

Learning with ICT can provide added value in extending learning opportunities for children, often in ways that only an ICT resource can offer. Such encounters can take place in all areas of the curriculum.

ICT used with young children will be most effective if the distinctive nature of development in the early years is taken into account. The importance of play, the quality of relationships with other children and adults, and meaningful learning contexts are all central to the high-quality learning experiences we provide. In selecting ICT resources for young children, factors such as robustness and mobility of equipment, choice of input devices, quality of feedback and other design features should be taken into account (Plowman and Stephen (ii), 2003).

In summary:

- children will vary in their experiences of and awareness of ICT prior to their starting in an early years setting
- children are generally curious about ICT and have a desire to explore different technologies
- multimedia and interactive resources can be especially motivating
- the potential to individualise many ICT resources fits well with the wide range of learning styles, interests, experiences and skills of young learners
- there is potential for children to learn with, about and through ICT
- ICT resources should reflect the distinctive nature of young children and their learning.

Principles

The principles underpinning the ICT policy framework build on the principles set out in the *Curriculum Framework for Children 3 to 5*, which are:

- the best interests of children
- the central importance of relationships
- the need for all children to feel included
- an understanding of the ways in which children learn.

The ICT policy framework principles can be expressed in the following ways.

Understanding the different ways in which children learn, and how information and communications technology is only one of a range of learning tools that can support this learning.

Relationships and interactions lie at the heart of all learning experiences including those involving information and communications technology.

Inclusion is promoted through a rich and varied information and communications technology environment.

All children can access a range of appropriate information and communications technology within their early years setting.

Understanding the different ways in which children learn, and how information and communications technology is only one of a range of learning tools that can support this learning.

The benefits that ICT can bring are already being seen in settings across Europe. Experiences both here and abroad have demonstrated that carefully selected ICT resources such as digital cameras and programmable toys can develop and extend young children's learning sometimes in original ways. This will most effectively be achieved when knowledge of young children's learning informs how information and communications technologies are selected, planned for, used and evaluated. The early years setting promotes children's learning across all aspects of the curriculum and it is important therefore that information and communications technologies are embedded within the learning environment, and not seen as separate entities. There should be no presumption that ICT, by its nature, will always offer a better tool for learning. Young children's active learning takes place in contexts that are meaningful to them. Staff should be able to make informed choices about how and when to use ICT.

Relationships and interactions lie at the heart of all learning experiences including those involving information and communications technology.

Young children learn effectively in collaboration with other children and adults. The use of information and communications technologies therefore should reflect this by encouraging children to develop shared understandings with other capable children or adults. Adults who are confident in the use of ICT will be able to interact with children in ways that will most effectively promote their learning and the development of their self-esteem.

Inclusion is promoted through a rich and varied information and communications technology environment.

Inclusion benefits all children and helps to promote equal opportunities to learn and develop in the ways that best suit them as unique individuals. ICT has the potential for being finely differentiated and providing individualised, sensitive feedback; therefore it can be particularly effective in helping to close the opportunity gap for children with additional support needs. Children with additional support needs can also benefit from different access strategies such as touch screens and switches. Individual children will be motivated and encouraged by different forms of ICT. It is important therefore that ICT use is also sensitive to the differences of gender and cultural and language backgrounds. ICT can be used as a tool for increasing diversity in early years settings, for instance by promoting different languages. The increased use of ICT in early years can help to close the 'digital divide' and ensure that all young children have access to technologies which are part of their world, both now and in the future.

All children can access a range of appropriate information and communications technology within their early years setting.

Resources for children should be wide-ranging and varied, reflecting the range of technologies available. Resources available should be selected with the particular needs of young children in mind, and are therefore likely to be present in all areas of the early years setting. Planning of all resources is important, particularly resources such as desktop computers and interactive whiteboards that by their static nature are less easily integrated throughout the learning environment.

Based on the principles identified for the use of ICT with young children, the implementation of this policy framework will require working towards the following aims.

- Aim 1: To develop pedagogy and practice in the use of ICT
- Aim 2: To reflect and promote equality and inclusive practice
- Aim 3: To ensure all children have access to, and the opportunity to learn about and with information and communications technology
- Aim 4: To develop, fund, and support professional development for all staff

Aim 1:

To develop pedagogy and practice in the use of ICT

The pedagogy concerning the use of ICT in early years in Scotland (and indeed elsewhere) needs to be further developed. Basing ICT use on the development of good practice and an evolving pedagogy, rather than allowing technology itself to drive progress, is an important aim of this policy framework. In order to further develop pedagogy various factors need to be considered.

Effective pedagogy

Research suggests that young children can learn effectively if adults take account of the importance of:

- developing an in-depth knowledge of each child as an individual
- self-initiated and self-directed learning, and the importance of intrinsic motivation
- children developing their understanding of the world through co-construction, by their interactions with other children and adults
- adults interacting sensitively to help children take their next steps in learning
- adults listening and asking questions to help children think about how they and other children learn
- feelings and emotions in learning
- the role of adult guided interactions in promoting young children's learning (Siraj-Blatchford et al., 2002; Stephen and Plowman, 2003).

Staff members need to engage in a reflective process if they are to use ICT to its greatest potential. They need to ask themselves about the value of the ICT resources that they are using. Software resources also can be subjected to similar questions, if ICT is to be used effectively to promote children's learning and development. Software evaluation services can help (ref. 10) but early years staff members need to be aware of the implicit assumptions about children's learning that inform development of software packages.

In further developing effective pedagogy, adults should:

- develop practice for helping children to learn as they use an ICT resource alone or with others
- value and act on children's choices
- think critically about their own role in promoting individual children's learning
- develop procedures for planning, observing and recording children's use of ICT.

ICT across the curriculum

A wider range of resources is now becoming more commonly available though not yet in early years settings. ICT resources can be used to impact on children's learning in all areas of the curriculum. At present many computer resources concentrate on literacy and numeracy. However the use of resources such as floor robots and toys can be incorporated into opportunities for problem solving and cooperation. Similarly, ICT resources such as old mobile phones, computer keyboards and so on, can present creative learning experiences to enhance imaginative play. Role play with ICT can support children in developing literacy and numeracy skills, as well as promoting personal and social development. The relationships between ICT literacy and other literacies need to be considered.

In order to work towards this aim we need to:

*   select resources in accordance with knowledge of children's development

*   reflect children's individual preferences in the use of ICT

*   use developing pedagogy and practice to seek ways of incorporating the best use of technology across all curriculum areas

*   plan for staff deployment taking into account ways in which adults can interact with children who are using ICT

*   incorporate planning, observing and recording children's use of ICT into present practices

*   have time to reflect on current use of ICT

*   participate in the ongoing debate about the usefulness of ICT for young children

*   develop additional support materials and further exemplification of the *Curriculum Framework for Children 3 to 5*

*   be more aware of the wide variety of ICT resources that are available

*   evaluate software more fully from a pedagogical standpoint.

Aim 2:
To reflect and promote equality and inclusive practice

An inclusive approach is a key characteristic of high-quality early years provision for young children and their families. This includes valuing the different experiences that children bring from home, and the contributions of parents.[4]

Different contexts for ICT

There are many contexts in which children are involved with ICT other than in their early years setting, for instance at home, with parents and siblings, and with their friends. Young children will enter their early years setting with varying awareness of and interest in ICT. Parents have a vital role to play as prime educators of young children and some children will have many achievements at home using ICT that can be celebrated and built on. Young children and their families may access learning available in the community, for instance community networks, libraries and learning centres, well before entry to early years establishments. Some parents will have developed ICT skills and knowledge that can usefully be shared with the early years setting. Consideration can also be given to offering parents who do not have access to computers at home opportunities for further learning. There is a need therefore to recognise that ICT can offer opportunities to promote partnerships between parents and staff. The potential of e-mail and intranets to improve communications between parents and centre, centre and centre, and in promoting continuity and progression at early years – P1 transition is clear. Spark,[5] the Scottish schools national intranet, could be of particular importance here. There is also potential for the early years setting to become part of a local 'connected community' where that exists, and to look further afield in developing links at national or even global levels.

Ensuring inclusive provision

An important aspect of ICT resources is their potential for promoting inclusion. ICT can offer enhanced access strategies for children with additional support needs and can also be individualised to meet their needs. ICT can be highly motivating and can help to break a cycle of disengagement for some children. It is important when selecting software to take into account gender, English as an additional language and provision in another language medium for instance Gaelic. Good practice will entail the use of software that cultivates and values diversity. Concern about the 'digital divide' has clear implications for equitable access to ICT in early years settings, particularly for those children who have limited access at home. Resources and access strategies can also provide social interactions, success and enjoyment for all children. More information for staff regarding such resources would aid planning for learning experiences.

Learning styles and dispositions

There is a growing interest in the varied ways in which young children approach learning experiences. Some children may find working with ICT particularly rewarding in comparison to non-ICT resources. Staff members know that children vary in their learning styles and in the different ways they solve problems. Similarly, children may have different dispositions; some are inclined to be more curious or investigative than others, some have more

---

[4] 'Parents' has been used to include parents and carers.
[5] See the NGfL annual report 2002 for discussion about the creation of a national Scottish schools intranet.

social orientations. These examples of diversity should be respected and have implications for the selection of resources and for the staff's planned interactions with children. It is important that staff members promote and encourage positive learning dispositions in children by respecting preferences and choices.

Continuity of learning opportunities

For some groups of children for instance Gypsy and Traveller children, children who are 'looked after and accommodated' and asylum seekers, the continuity of learning may be disrupted. ICT can offer opportunities to reduce the impact of these discontinuities on children's learning and development. In addition, some children may be quite separated from their cultural heritage. The use of ICT can be considered both as a tool for sharing information electronically and also for accessing information from the internet to support cultural identities.

In order to work towards this aim we need to:

- recognise, value and use children's experience of ICT outside the early years setting as an important learning resource
- take up the new opportunities that ICT can offer to become involved in partnership with parents and with local and wider communities
- support and value cultural identities and diversity by an appropriate use of the internet
- provide more information and support about the range of resources that can be particularly effective in promoting inclusive practice
- provide information and support about the use of ICT to support children's individual learning styles
- maximise the potential for using ICT to support continuity in children's learning.

Aim 3:

To ensure all children have access to, and the opportunity to learn about and with, information and communications technology

Within Scotland all 3- and 4-year-old children whose parents wish it, have the right to a place in an early years centre. The diversity of early years settings across the sectors of local authority, private and voluntary providers, provides parents and children with choices that best meet their needs and take into account the changing circumstances that are often a feature in the lives of families with young children. Different settings will develop and acquire their own range of ICT and other resources, best suited to their own individual context, and to the needs of their children. However, the varied nature of this universal provision means that it is especially important to ensure that all children have access to ICT resources and opportunities to use these to enhance their learning.

The development of this policy framework has been informed partly by an extensive consultation of all early years settings, results of which are detailed in the appendix to this paper. Implications for future developments in ICT resourcing are as follows.

Types of resources

There is an increasing availability of computer software and hardware, and a wide range of other old and new technologies, some of which have already been used effectively in early years settings for many years, for instance audio–visual equipment. It is important however that the wide range that is available is reflected within early years settings, and that, in particular, the use of desktop computers is not overemphasised. Resources should be selected taking into account the distinctive nature of development in the early years, and also the needs and requirements of individual settings.

Children's opportunities for learning

Diversity of provision in the early years sector leads to particular challenges in order to ensure equality of access for all children. Including all partners with an interest in young children in the development of integrated strategies for the early years has implications for how we make sure that all children access opportunities to learn with ICT.

For the use of ICT in the voluntary sector, issues relating to storage require to be considered. For many settings, for instance nursery classes and voluntary provision, appropriate access to the internet is not always available for children to use within the setting. Running costs of ICT, for instance cost of printer cartridges, can prohibit the use of ICT resources. In addition, there are some health and safety issues that need to be addressed in a more systematic way, for instance computer furniture and internet access. Technical support in many early years settings at present is variable. One aim of this policy framework is to encourage staff to plan more systematically for ICT use, and with this in mind, technical support is part of ensuring children's opportunities for learning. It is important for technical support services to be proactive rather than reactive, and to be made available to the whole range of early years settings. Local and national intranets will be most effective in promoting children's learning if they are extended to all settings.

In order to work towards this aim we need to:

- take into account the distinctive nature of development in the early years when selecting resources
- become familiar with the wide-ranging types of ICT that can be used with young children
- plan how best to provide equitable provision of a wider range of ICT resources
- include all early years settings in intranets and networking possibilities, particularly Spark
- put into place technical support arrangements for the early years sector
- identify running costs budgets for ICT consumables
- support the voluntary sector in identifying the best ways of overcoming storage and internet access difficulties
- widen the range of appropriate software available in early years settings
- produce health and safety guidelines relating to the use of ICT
- ensure that internet access is available for appropriate use by all children.

Aim 4:

To develop, fund and support professional development for all staff

The diversity of early years provision is reflected also in the varied professional development and training opportunities that staff members have been able to access in terms of ICT. The results of LT Scotland's national consultation concerning professional development needs of staff are considered in detail in the appendix to this paper.

The increased role of ICT in early years however presents new opportunities to review and evaluate the training needs of all staff. There is a need to consider how well professional development in the use of ICT is incorporated into the initial training of all prospective early years staff.

Professional development

Staff training requirements will be diverse, ranging from those staff in need of skills in basic computer and technology knowledge to other staff hoping to develop more varied or advanced learning. There is a need for a variety of delivery models to support this professional development.

Key requirements have been identified:

- Existing knowledge, experience and skills should be recognised and built on.
- There is a need to promote professional development in both pedagogy and practice of ICT to enhance its use within the early years context.
- Staff should be supported in their evaluation of hardware and software resources and to become more discerning in choosing appropriate resources within the early years context.
- Professional development in the area of ICT, as with the use of other resources, will require time for staff to reflect on, and share experiences with colleagues.
- Additional staff development material for ICT based on the *Curriculum Framework 3 to 5* should be developed.

Continuous professional development

The role of ICT with young children is likely to be a changing one, as new technologies are developed that will require different skills and aptitudes, and different challenges for pedagogy and practice. Alongside the ever-changing nature of ICT within the early years setting and the advancing technologies that staff will need to familiarise themselves with, the turnover of early years staff will also need to be considered. In order to sustain and support the processes of identifying and evaluating these changes, professional development will need to continually evolve. It will be necessary to ensure that delivery models are designed to reflect staff needs and, in turn, effectively support children's learning.

The wider context for workforce development

The Scottish Executive has a number of priorities for the early years and childcare workforce, forming the backdrop against which ICT training should be undertaken. The main priorities are to: increase the number of qualified workers; expand the workforce and widen opportunities for training; encourage both progression up the career ladder, and also lateral movement across the early years and childcare sector as a whole; and encourage diversity among the workforce that better reflects society. An equal importance is given to the acquisition of accredited qualifications and the undertaking of continuous professional development.

In order to work towards this aim we need to:

- use existing skills, knowledge and expertise to develop ways of incorporating ICT across the curriculum
- consider how best to provide continuous professional development on the value and use of ICT
- develop support materials that reflect both the needs of the early years sector and the different contexts of early years provision
- make sure that initial training for early years staff includes ICT training and awareness of ICT use embedded in the curriculum
- provide staff development that will:
  - develop basic skills by using a variety of delivery methods with a range of entry points
  - promote continuous professional development in the use of ICT
- ensure that the content and delivery of materials and courses have a pedagogical emphasis.

Conclusion

Rapid advances in ICT are likely to continue, so that its role in early years will itself be changing and fluid. In two, three or four years time, ICT in early years settings is likely to be quite different from at present. An important theme of this policy framework has therefore been to value the work of early years staff, and to highlight the continued professional development that will be necessary to support, enhance and further develop young children's learning using information and communications technologies in the future. It is hoped that the opportunities for professional development and support materials combine with this policy framework to drive progress forward.

There is an identified enthusiasm, interest and commitment among early years staff for using ICT to promote the learning and development of young children. The process of monitoring and evaluation that goes along with the strategy will ensure this momentum is developed so that ICT becomes an integral part of learning in the early years. By getting it right in the early years, ICT can contribute to ensuring the best possible start in life for all children.

Appendix: Development of the Strategy

Learning and Teaching Scotland was asked by the Scottish Executive in October 2001 to carry out a review of the role of ICT in pre-school. During 2001/2, the following action was taken.

- A commissioned literature review (Stephen and Plowman, 2002)
- A consultation with local authorities and external agencies that was also available online at www.LTScotland.com/earlyyears
- A commissioned study of current practice in ICT in a number of early years settings (Stephen and Plowman, 2003)
- An extensive national consultation of all early years settings, including Partner Providers and voluntary organisations, also available to complete online (Fraser et al., 2003, unpublished). This consultation attracted responses comparable in number to others undertaken by LT Scotland. It should however be borne in mind that this is still a minority sample; it is possible that the results may overestimate both the level of staff expertise and the availability of resources.

The results of this review can be summarised as follows.

General themes

- There is a scarcity of good-quality research findings on using ICT in educational settings for young children, and little evidence to support either the claims made for its benefits, or the warnings about potential harm. Thus there are many questions that remain unanswered in relation to the benefits of the use of ICT by young children.
- Staff members on the whole are enthusiastic about the use and potential value of ICT in their work. They are keen to build on and develop their professional expertise in this area. There is an identified need among staff both for professional development and support and also for a pedagogical debate about ICT use, for example why and how to use ICT.

- There are variations throughout Scotland in:
  - children's access to appropriate ICT resources
  - children's different preferences and choices for using ICT
  - the availability of resources in different settings and sectors
  - staff skills and levels of confidence in using ICT.

Current practice

Results of the study of current practice (Stephen and Plowman, 2003) suggest that:

- ICT use in early years settings is rarely part of explicit planning
- observing and recording children's ICT use is not common practice at present
- staff members tend not to interact in a planned way with children using the computer
- there is therefore little scope for reflection on children's use of ICT
- there is a belief that young children learn computer skills almost automatically and with little effort

- staff members are mostly positive about the benefits of ICT use with young children, but with little evidence from practice to support this belief
- observations of children working with the computer however, demonstrate that not all interactions with computers (as with other resources) are supportive of children's learning.

Skills and professional development

- Only about 10 per cent of staff members have ICT expertise described as either excellent or good, with the skills of half of all staff described as basic or inadequate. Over a third had not attended any ICT training in the past two years. Of those who had attended courses, most had been concerned with basic skills or word processing. Although basic skills are still a necessity for many staff, accessing multimedia software is the most frequently identified training need.
- Half of the staff members that responded to the consultation have access to internet and e-mail at work, but only 15 per cent have this available for children to use. This lack of internet access is likely to be because access is only available in a separate part of the building.
- The most common use of ICT within early years settings is that of multimedia software, for example CD-ROMs. Some staff however also used ICT to assist in record keeping and assessment.
- An important aspect of professional development was an increase in staff confidence using ICT.

ICT resources

- The early years sector has not had the same planned, sustained and substantial funding for ICT that has been available in the primary and secondary sectors, so that little information has been available concerning children's access to ICT resources in their early years setting.
- Most settings have a small number of computers, although these vary in age and operating system. CD-ROM software is the most common use for computers, although a number of settings use the computer for various kinds of record keeping and assessment tasks. Half of the settings have a digital camera. Similar numbers have access to the internet, although this includes nursery classes where the children themselves may not have access. Very few have other ICT resources, for example programmable toys.
- It seems clear therefore that not all children have equitable access to resources. The challenge is therefore to ensure the entitlement of all children to this, especially within the context of integrated services for children.
- The same concerns relate to internet access, networking potential and other aspects of infrastructure.

Strategy development

The information gathered by Learning and Teaching Scotland has been used to inform the development of an ICT strategy for early years (Plowman and Stephen (i), 2003).

A national steering group will oversee the implementation of the strategy.

References

1. Condie, R, Simpson, M, Payne, F and Gray, D, *Insight2 – The Impact of ICT Initiatives in Scottish Schools*, Scottish Executive, 2002 www.scotland.gov.uk/library5/education/ins2-00.asp

2. DfES/Becta, *ImpaCT 2, The Impact of Information and Communication Technologies on Pupil Learning and Attainment*, Schools Research and Evaluation Series, 7, 2002 www.becta.org.uk/research/reports/docs/ImpaCT2_strand1_report.pdf

3. Fraser, H, O'Hara, P and Stead, J, *The Role of ICT in Pre-School Education*, Final Report on LT Scotland's September 2002 Consultation, 2003 (unpublished)

4. Harris, S and Kington, A, *Innovative Classroom Practices using ICT in England – Implications for Schools*, NFER, 2002

5. Plowman, L and Stephen, C (i), 'Using research to inform policy: ICT and pre-school education in Scotland', Invited Paper (2pp) for Early Learning in the Information Society: A European Conference. Hosted by IBM, Brussels, May 2003. Contact lydia.plowman@stir.ac.uk for electronic copy.

6. Plowman, L and Stephen, C (ii), 'A "Benign Addition?". A review of research on ICT with pre-school children', *Journal of Computer Assisted Learning*, vol. 19, no. 2, pp. 149–164, 2003 www.ioe.stir.ac.uk/CACHET/publications.htm

7. Scottish Consultative Council on the Curriculum, *A Curriculum Framework for Children 3 to 5*, Dundee: Scottish Consultative Council on the Curriculum, 1999

8. Scottish Executive, Progress Report 2, NGfL Scotland, 2002 www.scotland.gov.uk/library5/education/nglm-00.asp

9. Siraj-Blatchford, I, Sylva, K, Muttock, Gilden, R and Bell, D, *Researching Effective Pedagogy in the Early Years*, Research Report 356, DfES, London, 2002

10. Software evaluation sites
    *   www.ictadvice.org
    *   www.ltscotland.org.uk/softpub/evaluations.asp
    *   http://besd.becta.org.uk
    *   www.pin.org.uk/
    *   www.teem.org.uk/

11. Stephen, C and Plowman L, *ICT in Pre-School: A 'Benign Addition?'*, Learning and Teaching Scotland, 2002

12. Stephen, C and Plowman L, *'Come back in two years!', a study of the use of ICT in pre-school settings during spring and summer 2002*, Learning and Teaching Scotland, 2003

Learning and Teaching Scotland, Gardyne Road, Dundee DD5 1NY Tel: 01382 443600 Fax: 01382 443645/6

Learning and Teaching Scotland, 74 Victoria Crescent Road, Glasgow G12 9JN Tel: 0141 337 5000 Fax: 0141 337 5050

www.LTScotland.org.uk   e: enquiries@LTScotland.org.uk

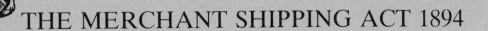

DEPARTMENT OF TRANSPORT

THE MERCHANT SHIPPING ACT 1894

mv HERALD OF FREE ENTERPRISE

Report of Court No. 8074.

Formal Investigation

London
Her Majesty's Stationery Office
£10.50 net

63-
23
94

ER

ASTON UNIVERSITY

LIBRARY & INFORMATION SERVICES

Aston Triangle
Birmingham
B4 7ET
England

Tel: 021 359 3611
Fax: 021 359 7358